Life, Love and MEMORIES

JAMES A. CARNRIGHT

authorHOUSE®

AuthorHouse™
1663 Liberty Drive, Suite 200
Bloomington, IN 47403
www.authorhouse.com
Phone: 1-800-839-8640

© 2008 James A. Carnright. All rights reserved.

No part of this book may be reproduced, stored in a retrieval system, or transmitted by any means without the written permission of the author.

First published by AuthorHouse 6/23/2008

ISBN: 978-1-4343-8703-5 (sc)

Printed in the United States of America
Bloomington, Indiana

This book is printed on acid-free paper.

Forward

I have been retired some twenty years now, and have reached the "ripe" old age of eighty seven. In my lifetime I've graduated from the University of Alabama, followed by three years of service in World War II. Soon after being discharged, I courted and married, Emily, on the 29th of September 1949. We had three wonderful children, Diane, James, Jr. and last but not least, John. The poems that follow touch on my life, my family, my philosophy on life, seasons of the year, holidays and a smattering of humor. I hope you will enjoy reading them as much as I have enjoyed writing them.

DEDICATION

I dedicate this book of poems posthumously to Emily, my dear wife of fifty years.

TABLE OF CONTENTS

Chapter I My Life 7

Chapter II Family and Friends 33

Chapter III My Philosophy on Life 55

Chapter IV Seasons and Holidays 79

Chapter V A Smattering of Humor. 97

CHAPTER I
MY LIFE

My Life
Olio
The Autumn of My Life
'Till Death Did Us Part
Love Letters
Love Letters Straight From Her Heart
Alabama The Beautiful
Delaware Blue Hens
How Sweet It Is?
World War II
First Presbyterian Church
At-Last-A Camp
My Delaware

My Life

Well…..here I am at 85
and feel damn lucky to be alive.

"In the beginning" seems a good way to start,
but biblically I'm years apart.

Even so, time flies by,
year after year in the blink of an eye.

More reason to make your journey worth while,
and while you're at it, do it in style.

It's easy to tell when you're an old fellow,
your zipper is rusty and your sneakers are yellow.

That rhymes pretty well but not too mellow,
you can tell the following poems weren't written by
Longfellow!

I've lived a wonderful life,
thanks to good parents and a fantastic wife.

We were blessed with children, one girl, two boys,
and together they gave us so many joys.

I'm in my "twilight" so they say,
but before I go I want to pray……

"Lord God as one of your sheep,
please take me home while I'm in my sleep".

OLIO*
(* A Miscellaneous Mixture)

I was born at home, July 7, 1920.
Mother was there, of course, as well as
the doctor and my Dad.
That made three for company and that's not too bad.

The other day someone called me "home boy",
and I thought to myself, how did he know?
He had to be a psychic with an attitude in tow.

Experiences in life can be like that,
especially when you're just "chewing the fat".
Conversations can, at times, be cruel,
and when they are, silence, on your part,
is the "Golden Rule".

Growing up is hard to do.
You have homework in school and in making
friends you must be "cool".
And be sure you make the right kind of friends—
don't be a fool.

Prepare yourself in mind and body so you can
compete successfully in whatever you do.
Who knows, you might end up with your name
listed in the famous, "Who's Who".

In your lifetime, strive to be good, not evil,
be thoughtful of others,
for on this Earth we are all sisters and brothers.

THE AUTUMN OF MY LIFE

I love you Lord, what can I say,
you've been with me all the way.
You gave me a brain and opportunities
to enhance it.
You gave me courage so, at times,
I could chance it.

You gave me a bride like no other on earth,
and three children we could enjoy since their birth.

You've given me so many blessings,
I'm almost embarrassed to count,
and yet at 85 they continue to mount.

To thank you, God, I'm at a loss for words,
but I know you can understand.
Just as throughout my entire life,
you've given me your hand.

I've lived a happy and productive life,
with a girl named Emily,
my love, my friend and my dear wife.

Now, in the autumn of my years,
I have no tears,
I have no regrets....
life for me, Lord, has been as good as it gets!

'Till Death Did Us Part

Seems like the longer I live,
the more I become aware of the fact that
the marriage Emily and I had was one in a million.
It's foundation was based on commitment, fun and love,
a perfect match of two human beings
made in Heaven above.
For fifty years it was nothing short of total bliss,
each day ending in a tender kiss.

It's now been eight years since God called Emily home
and for me, time has taken it's toll.
I currently am using a "walker" and soon a wheelchair,
but hey, there's a bright side, I still have most of my hair!

Now, when I'm in the bathroom to shave,
I can't help noticing
the aging process that's taken place,
and I say to myself, "I'd hate to have Emily see me now".
And yet, deep down in my heart,
I know that if through some act of God,
she came back to me,
we would both look as beautiful in each others eyes
as we did from the very start!

LOVE LETTERS

My life began and ended with just two little words:
Emily saying, "I do"
and the nurse saying to me, "She's gone"
The years too have come and gone,
but I do my best to carry on.

I've saved your many love letters, Em,
although at times, I can't be sure what for.
I guess it was because they were sent to me,
by the angel that I adored.

Now that you have passed away,
I read one or two, now and then,
just to make my day.

I was reading one a short while ago, Em,
"if only you could realize how deeply I love
every part of you. There isn't a soul who
could ever come before you in my heart.
It's so wonderful to know that we will
have each other forever….almost too beautiful."

It's these memories I hold so dear,
and they've uplifted me year after year.

To think God arranged for you and me to meet,
fall in love and dedicate our lives to each other,
is nothing short of a miracle,
followed by another and yet another.

I'm terribly lonesome, Em, our vibrant
home is now so stark.
I don't know what I'll do
when I can't hear Annie's bark.

Love Letters Straight From Her Heart
To Diane, Jimmy & John

Before I met your mother, which is synonymous with before my life began, there were 29 years consisting of a wonderful childhood, grade school, high school, college and a 3 year hitch in the Army.

Em's and my first meeting, precluded any need for a second!
The love letters she wrote to me, prior to our marriage, were so beautiful that I've saved many from that time until the present – a span of 55 years.
I'm sure she wouldn't mind me sharing a few excerpts with you............

"If only you could realize how deeply I love every part of you. There isn't a soul who could ever come before you in my heart."

"And I need you so much, Jim. I don't feel whole when we're apart. I can't imagine going through life without you."

"Did I say you were good for me?
For better or for worse, you're my whole future..
I can't conceive of life without you, Jim."

There are 20 letters in all, but I must end here for I've run out of tears. Just a final note to my Emily..
The success of our marriage was based on
the fact that we were:
So much the same
So much in love

So anxious to please
So dedicated to each other
So much in love
So much the same

As someone once said,
"When you lose a loved one by death,
the hurt lasts forever."

ALABAMA THE BEAUTIFUL

There's a football team with lots of pride.
They're known nationwide as the "Crimson Tide".
It's a marvelous history we all have to share,
but it's not complete without the "Bear".

The "Million Dollar Band" is the finest in the land.
They're half time shows deserve a big hand.
Whenever they play "Yea Alabama",
I want to jump to my feet and shout hosanna.

Cheerleaders are always good for your soul.
They pep you up to attain your goal.
They encourage cheering of course.
The results of which can leave you hoarse.

Our beloved "Big Al" is the size of a house
but definitely not afraid of a mouse.
He can lift the team's spirit but not with his trunk.
As the girls would say, he's really a "hunk".

Whenever it comes to "push or shove",
the "Crimson Tide" will rise above.

ROLL TIDE!

Delaware Blue Hens

When the Blue & Gold band plays "Delaware",
my spirit goes soaring into the air.

Tubby Raymond and "Bear" Bryant are legends in time.
They'll both live on' cause their records shine.

"U Dee" and "Big Al" are mascots supreme.
They contribute to the game and inspire the team.

My best friend, Ted, is a rabid fan.
He's had season tickets since God knows when.

The guy who wrote this poem is an Alabama alumnus.
If you missed the clues, "you missed the bus"!

How Sweet It Is!?

Living with Diabetes is a monumental feat,
most food you love, you can no longer eat.
Drinks as well are "under the gun",
which denies you of those that used to be fun.
Pertaining to a Diabetes diet, there is no doubt,
if it tastes good, just spit it out!

Making up a menu low in carbs is easier
said than done.......
you must read background information, study
charts and labels before you can say you've won.

Diabetes has had a weird effect on me....
songs like "Sweet Adeline", "Sweetheart"
and "Sweeter than Springtime" now give me chills,
where previously they played a big part
in helping me cure my ills.

Looking back on my life, I recall a dog of mine
named "Sugar". Today, it's a shame, for according
to my Diabetes agenda, I'd have no other choice
but to call her "Splenda". How sad!

WORLD WAR II

A Three Part Chronological Poem

CHRONOLOGY

The War began on September 1, 1939 when Germany attacked Poland.
By early 1942 all major countries of the world were involved.
The Allies mobilized 62 million men and women. The Axis; Germany, Italy and Japan, mobilized about half that number.

PART 1

"The Battle For Eastern Europe And Great Britain"

PART 2

"America Enters The War"

PART 3

"The Liberation of Europe"

WWII – Part 1
"The Battle For Eastern Europe and Great Britain"

There is absolutely nothing glorious about a war.
It's nothing but sacrifice and gore.
WWI was "the war to end all wars"..so how come WWII?
If you read your history books you'll discover what is true.

After the first war was won, the Versailles Treaty was blamed a lot,
for stripping Germany of all they got.
Out of this suppression came unrest,
which Adolph Hitler exploited with zest.

He rose to power by promising the German people a place in the sun.
He formed the "Nazi" party and in time all citizens were "under the gun".
Jews were despised, placed in concentration camps for ultimate annihilation.
Millions were gassed and died from asphyxiation.

Like all dictators, hungry for power,
he invaded European nations which he ultimately devoured.
First Poland, Austria, Czechoslovakia and France,
then the others when he had the chance.

In time, Hitler was smitten,
to wage outright war against Great Britain.
He unleashed his Luftwaffe and V-2 Rockets on London.

German submarines (U-Boats), as well,
were sinking supply ships
in an added effort to give them hell.
It was in those days, that the outnumbered RAF (Royal Air Force),
inflicted heavy losses on the Luftwaffe
whenever they came in view.
All this inspired Prime Minister Winston Churchill's famous quotation…
"Never have so many owed so much to so few."

WWII – PART 2
"AMERICA ENTERS THE WAR"

PROLOGUE

About 7:55 a.m., December 7, 1941 (Hawaii time), about 360 Japanese planes bombed Pearl Harbor and on July 8th, President Franklin Delano Roosevelt declared war on Japan. He called December 7th, "A date which will live in* infamy."

(*infamy – evil reputation brought about by something grossly criminal, shocking or brutal)

This poem could never cover all the battles and sacrifices that our G.I.'s, sailors, marines and airmen endured. Heroism too, became the norm, leading America to ultimate victory.

Destruction at Pearl Harbor was widespread,
while many servicemen were still asleep in their bed.
With battle ships sunk and planes destroyed,
it left our defenses with a terrible void.

During this "down time", Japanese invaded the Philippines,
forcing Gen. McArthur to escape by sea as he watched Manila burn.
It was, at this time, he spoke these immortal words…
"I shall return."

Success in the Pacific war was not measured by ground covered,
but island by island as we discovered.

Japanese were hidden in caves with deep tunnels down lower
and marines snuffed them out by the use of flame throwers.

Stepping stones to victory were the re-taking of the Philippines,
followed by island hopping that brought us closer to Japan with each one.*

*Major islands re-taken were: Midway, Guadalcanal, Tarawa, Kwajalein and Saipan.

All of this could not have been done
without the U.S. Navy sinking Japanese battleships and
aircraft carriers, forcing them to run.

The most decisive naval engagement
was the Battle of the Coral Sea.
It raged on for four days,
and established United States supremacy.

For the Japanese it was a fateful day,
when the Atomic bomb was dropped on Hiroshima
by the "Enola Gay".
Several days later, it was Nagasaki,
forcing the Japanese to surrender to survive,
on September, 2, 1945.

WWII – Part 3
"The Liberation of Europe"

Prologue

The Allies assembled a force of almost 3,000,000 men and stored 16,000,000 tons of arms, munitions and supplies in Britain for the great invasion. The Allies had 5,000 large ships, 4,000 landing craft and more than 11,000 aircraft.

To set the scene, all of Europe had been
in bondage for a number of years.
The gross human suffering would
bring anyone to tears.
The Nazi's Hitler was a psychopath at best,
but truthfully speaking, compared to Stalin of Russia,
and Mussolini of Italy, he was not much worse than the rest.

D-Day

When the Allied invasion approached Omaha Beach,
there was a flotilla of ships as far as the eye could
reach.

Paratroopers and gliders had already attained their
goal,
to secure roads and bridges,
thereby putting German defenders in a hole.

American "GI's", "Brits" and "Canadians" made up
the attacking force of this successful invasion....
Berlin, Germany was it's final destination.

The Allies advanced West, village by village,
freeing Paris, then on to the Rhine with very little time
for pillage.

The German "Panzer" tanks were awesome.
Our tanks were normally in trouble whenever they saw
some.
Fortunately for the Allies, as time would pass,
the Germans literally ran out of gas.

"The Battle of the Bulge" would be Germany's
last massive offensive. Although caught off guard,
the GI's made them pay dearly for every yard.
It was Winter and very cold,
but when we were asked to surrender, the German's
were told............"nuts!"
Soon the race for Berlin was on
and with great success,
we reached the city outskirts from the East
while the Russians approached from the West.

Gen. Eisenhower let the long suffering Russians take
the city,
which they gladly did without pity.
Hitler committed suicide in his underground bunker,
ending a regime of hatred, greed, torture and hunger.

More than 9,000,000 Allied servicemen died in the war.
After 60 years it still cries out,
"Thank you" to all who signed aboard!

First Presbyterian Church
(My home away from home)

First Church with it's white columns and
melodious spire,
is situated downtown for all to admire.
Within the sanctuary you will be able to see,
stain glass windows of glorious antiquity.

The beautiful sound of music swells,
from a dedicated and talented group ringing bells.
Talented organ and piano players too,
set the mood for worshipers in the pew.
And the songs that are sung by our choir,
is music you just can't help but admire.

I have come here to worship for more years
than I dare to say,
but it's always been, to me,
my favorite place to pray.

Ministers come and ministers go,
but God is still among us all, this I know!

AT-LAST-A Camp
(Dedicated to my Mother, Ethel, who started it all!)

In the Adirondacks there's a heaven on earth
that our children have known since their birth.

It's on Brant Lake with mountains in view.
The area so beautiful it gets to you.

The camp has been in the family for 66 years.
It has seen much joy and very few tears.

If fishing and swimming wind your clock,
you can do 'em both right off the dock.

It's been a spot for celebrations,
birthdays, holidays and yes, vacations.

Friends and family have come from near and far,
some by boat but mostly by car.

For our family it's been a gem.
It has appeal for all of them.

Children, grandchildren and great grandchildren too,
Brant Lake has become a family glue.

There is really no ending to this story.
"At-last-a" will live on in all her glory.

Amen.

My Delaware

If you don't like snow, sleet, tornados, forest fires,
mud slides, earthquakes or floods with cars floating
down the street,
then Delaware becomes the state that's impossible to beat!

If you don't like high property taxes in addition to sales tax,
just move to Delaware and you can finally relax....
we don't have either one.
If you can't stand to dwell in a large Metropolis,
Delaware is
devoid of them as well.

If you happen to like ocean bathing, ocean fishing,
bay, river or fresh lake fishing,
then this is the place you've been missing.

If you like hunting deer,
there are plenty here,
If you're fond of eating oysters or trapping "blue claw" crab,
you're lucky...you can eat all you can grab.

Delaware is the second smallest state in the U.S.A.,
and the first to sign the Declaration of Independence.
Because of it's size, all the wonderful aforementioned
amenities are as near as a short drive away.

Please excuse my obvious prejudice,
but out of all the states in the U.S.A.,
I'll take Delaware any old day!

CHAPTER II
FAMILY AND FRIENDS

Emily
My Diane
Keep On Truckin
Fishin and Wishin
Barbara
Christine
Alex's Career
A Poem To My Dog Annie
Nightly Prayer
A Poem in Memory of Annie
Reflections on My Dear Friend Bill
Zeb
Friend
Nancy
My Cousin Gilbert
Gone But Not Forgotten
Poncho and Lisa
Out With The Old – In With The New

EMILY

To Emily, my bride, my wife,
who stood beside me through married life.

During courtship, I said to my folks,
"This girl is special; she even laughs at my jokes".

Major issues were seldom a problem,
Em and I had so much in common.

Our relationship could not have been better,
'cause when push came to shove I usually let her.

We had children, we had fun, we had friends
and love to spare.
We had "heaven on earth" which is so very rare.

In essence we were two peas in a pod,
unmistakably put there by God.

I'm blessed by the children you bore for us....
not one, not two but three.
We'll all love you, honey, until eternity.

Oh, and Em, say hello to God for me.

My Diane

When you first joined your Mother and I,
we were so happy we could almost cry.

Freeport, Long Island was your place of birth,
and we showed you off for all we were worth.

From a little girl with curly blond hair,
you soon became a beautiful young woman with
charm to spare.

Your marriage to Perry was a highlight of your life,
when you two became man and wife.

Soon Perry, Jr. was born, then Amy too,
if you'd had many more you'd be living in a shoe!

Now Madison, Alex, Eric and Bryce have joined the crowd,
which makes each one of us very proud.

May good health and happiness be with us all,
and through our lives may we always stand tall.

Keep On Truckin

My son Jim's main intent,
is going to Lancaster and hauling cement.
He drives a powerful" rig",
I'll tell you that thing is really big.

How he maneuvers it in heavy traffic
is a mystery to me.
I guess you get the "hang of it"
before there's a catastrophe.

He drives six nights like a "work-a-holic",
which leaves little time for fun and frolic.
His wife, Barbara, is really the "tops"
and on Saturdays they love "destroying" the shops.

Driving like Jim does must be an awful grind,
which in time has to take a toll on the "behind".
He loves it though, which is great to hear,
but I'm still concerned about his "rear"!

Keep it up, Jim, you're doing fine,
and I'm proud that you're a son of mine.

FISHIN AND WISHIN

My son, John, bless his soul,
is happiest when he's holding a pole.
Early on, by hook or crook,
he soon learned how to bait his own hook.

As years passed by he got pretty good.
He'd catch fish near "structures" which I learned was sunken wood.

He'd say to me, "Pop, you said Brant Lake was all fished out."
Then he'd go catch a nice big trout.

John, I hate to admit when I'm seldom wrong and
this is certainly not my proverbial "Swan Song".
I now take pride when I see,
how successful you are with what you learned from me.

I had trouble getting fish to bite,
because I didn't watch "Nature Channel" the previous night.
OK, so that's an excuse as you can see,
we never even owned a darn T.V.

Fishing is a wonderful sport, it's relaxing and it's fun.
Every fish that's on your line, you swear it weighs a ton.

Cares seem to melt away,
when you're wetting a line on a beautiful day.

BARBARA
(My Daughter-In-Law)

Sometimes you're lucky, sometimes you're not,
in Barbara's case, I love what I got!

She's thoughtful, caring and kind.
Do me a favor? She doesn't mind.

She and my son were made for each other,
and are they in love? Oh, brother!

Barbara is an excellent cook who concocts
meals that please……..
That's providing she's got plenty of cheese!

Both she and Jim love to food shop,
infact, with enough coupons,
they'll shop till they drop.

Barbara, when you agreed to become
a Deacon of our church,
I could not have been more proud.
It's accepting responsibilities like this,
that sets you apart from the crowd!

There's an old saying, "Love me, love my dog"
that suits you, my dear, to a tee.
In short, what I'm trying to say, Barbara,
"you're the tops" with me!

CHRISTINE

As my problem with "vertigo" got worse and worse,
I made an appointment to see the doctor
before I required a hearse.

Whoever said "Don't leave a stone unturned",
must have been one of his peers or one of his clan.
In any case, he scheduled me for just about
every test except a bloody mammogram.

There was blood work at the hospital, a spinal
tap and an M.R.I.
How he left out a colonoscopy, I cannot tell you why.

In my condition, getting back and forth for all
these appointments put me in a difficult position.
God works in wondrous ways!
Some we can understand, but then, there are days.

I have been blessed so often it seems like a dream...
then in the flesh an angel came by and her name was
CHRISTINE!
She's cheerful, responsible and eager to please,
and for that I am so very grateful.
I can not imagine what I'd have done if she
had been hateful!

Alex's Career

Congratulations to Alex on his meteoric climb
Up the corporate ladder.
Unfortunately, this includes relocation from place to place,
For which you have to "bite the bullet" as if it didn't matter.

Constant moving can rattle anyone's nerves and
Involve many hours being spent.
Alex, my suggestion to you would be to trade
Your car for two camels and a tent!

A Poem To My Dog Annie

My dog and I are not too spry.
We're getting old and that is why.

We've been together for fifteen years,
and when she goes there'll be a flood of tears.

Emily gave Annie to me on our 40th Anniversary.
She had no idea what that little dog would mean to me.

There are many days when clouds get muddy.
Annie cheers me up cause she's my buddy.

She's loyal and loving in "hell or high water".
That's why to me, she's just like my daughter.

NIGHTLY PRAYER

Dear Lord God I pray,
let Annie live yet another day.

Like me she's getting very old,
but to me Lord God she's solid gold!

A Poem In Memory of Annie
January, 2006

Annie now resides in dog Heaven,
where there are beds of roses
and no cold noses.
There could not be a more wonderful place,
she's got bones to chew and squirrels to chase.

Annie has left a legacy of undying love and devotion,
from a heart that's the size of an ocean.
Since the day Emily gave her to me,
she immediately became a special member of our family.

Annie never met a human or another dog she didn't like.
She should have run for office,
'cause she'd do what it takes……
she's licked more hands than a politician shakes.

Her ears were an outstanding feature
that set her apart.
They gave her that certain charm which caused
one to take her to one's heart.

I know somewhere in the great beyond,
much farther than I can see,
I'll find Annie there, waiting just for me.

REFLECTIONS ON MY DEAR FRIEND BILL

Bill, our friendship went back 35 years at least.
If friendship was food, we really had a feast.

Your attributes were many, and to me, I would
list just a few; loyal, compassionate, unselfish and jolly.
I shall miss your wholehearted laugh,
whenever I told you a joke, by golly!

As far as being unselfish, Bill, you were a total
giving human being without exception.
I truly believe the saying, "ask and you shall receive",
had you in mind at it's conception.

Trouble with your car or mower?
No need to panic if Bill is your mechanic!
In your garage you had more tools than Sears
and about as many old parts as Fitzgeralds.
The tools were neatly kept in a special chest
or drawer, the parts were kept in barrels.

I used to tell people:
"If my buddy Bill can't fix it,
you might as well deep six it!"

You lived a very meaningful life,
during which time you brightened
many, many lives, including my own.
And now that we've come to an end,
I thank God for arranging you to be my friend.

ZEB

John's dog "Zeb" is a delight to have around,
he is as loving as he can be and hardly makes a sound.
In addition to "Zeb", he's also called "Buddy" and "Zebadoo",
but no matter what you may call him, he promptly comes to you.

Zeb is a lover at heart and likes you to rub his back and tummy.
If he could talk I know he'd tell you, the rubbing to him is just yummy.

Zeb is an obedient dog who John has taught well,
when you let him out the door he'll run "pell mell",
but as soon as he reaches the street, he stops on a dime,
and I mean every time!

During the day, he'll find a rug, especially if it's in the sun.
I believe he does this to build up energy for when John comes home. If John calls him "Buddy" and claps his hands,
this dog will explode, running circles around the house having super fun.

Zeb's other love is Christine, who cares for him all day while John's at work.
Zeb is a real blessing to John, Christine and me,
for without him there'd be a lot less glee!

FRIEND
(In Memory of Bob Dewalt)

My best friend Bob Dewalt,
was truly a man without a fault.

Well, what do you know,
having said that, my nose is beginning to grow.

Helen and Emily and Bob and I,
were great for each other, that's no lie.

While Bob and I played golf a lot,
Helen and Emily would shop till they dropped.

Bob to me was a generous soul,
except when he happened to lose a hole!

The premium business was his pride and joy.
He made, "I can get it for you wholesale" a terrific ploy.

With his wits he rose to the top of his game.
We're not talking golf now 'cause that's not the same.

When I think of a foursome that has shared more years of fun,
you can search the world over and find there are none.

NANCY

Nancy is my "Cuz",
the bestest "Cuz" there ever was!
Believe it or not I taught her to drive,
and I thank the dear Lord I'm still alive.

On one occasion, when we were together,
she took a fall landing unlike a feather.
From that memorable day on,
the appropriate name for her I put*,
you guessed it, "Sure Foot".

I know for certain, a highlight of her life was
when she met Tom, a most wonderful fella,
who turned her into the story book, Cinderella.
Tom was thoughtful, caring and his generosity did abound.
Adding to these attributes he was really fun to be around.

Nancy and I have both lost the "loves of our lives",
but we carry on with great memories to enjoy.
In wedding vows they include, "till death do us part".
They should read, "till death do us part and meet again
in heaven for a brand new start".

*Poetic license!

My Cousin Gilbert

I love my cousin Gilbert who's like a brother to me.
As young boys in Saugerties, we were together constantly.

You've never been "up the creek" until
you've been fishing up the Esopus.
Gil had a rowboat there and some "dude"
caught more fish than "bof-us" ….yea, right!

We had family outings on the speedboat, "Neewah",
with our parents to "Turkey Point".
There we swam in the Hudson, picnicked and it was
really a place where it didn't disappoint.

One time "Gilly" and I took his outboard up the
Hudson River from Saugerties to Albany.
We were not supposed to go that far, but
as mileage was concerned, we forgot how many.

This one "takes the cake"!
Gilbert and I rode on inner tubes out to the Hudson
River…waited for the Albany to New York Dayline to
come by just to ride it's wake!

Years later we continued to keep in touch….
WWII, marriage, children and such.
Although time has taken its toll on both of us,
we're happy for all the good times God has given us.

We are now in the twilight of our lives,
and have been blessed through it all with two
incredible parents and two incredible wives.

GONE BUT NOT FORGOTTEN
Dedicated to Abe and Ellen

Abe and Ellen are two wonderful people,
whose friendship I shall miss.
I trust their move from Milford
will provide them with much bliss.

Whenever they'd invite me to dine,
Abe made a great Manhattan and Ellen had her wine.
All of this was a prelude to a dinner
which was really fine.

Our conversations were not about x-rays and art,
for the simple reason I could not take part.
Abe liked stories and I as well,
so Ellen put up with both of us and never gave us hell!
Our stories were clean and mostly "corny",
but if they're funny it's another story.

Abe and Ellen….best wishes in your new location,
and may your continuing lives together be a great sensation!

PONCHO AND LISA

When Poncho and Lisa first lived in the
house across from me,
I never realized how wonderful that would be.
They're both thoughtful and kind...
ask for a favor and they don't mind.
Thank Poncho for problem solvin',
he'll simply reply, "It's no problem!"

Another "perk", originally unbeknownst to me,
was when they opened the
"friends and neighbors" drive-in eatery.
Grown ups and children of Colby's
generation where invited to attend,
with play yard units the kids enjoyed to no end.

I really don't know how Lisa finds the time to
shop and prepare such wonderful food.
She must spend half her day in the kitchen,
if not more,
ending up with food galore!

Poncho is the other player in the team of
Julia Childs and Emeril Lagasse.
Lisa cooks with the oven and stove top......
Poncho cooks on the outside grill, delivering
hamburgers almost non-stop.
Ann is her usual "good scout",
by bringing a dish or two, just to help out.

Colby, I'm sure, enjoys all the excitement
by friends of his age and acting like a boy.
He's a fine young man who's sure to
grow up to be his family's pride and joy!

OUT WITH THE OLD
IN WITH THE NEW

It's out with the old and in with the new...
a gorgeous home with a lakeside view,
and I've observed it being built,
from plans designed right up to the hilt.

To Poncho, Lisa and Ann I say,
"Welcome to your new home on this long awaited day."

Colby will have a ball with his own "pad"
so appealing....
it even includes a train suspended from the ceiling!

Lisa has a kitchen second to none,
where she can cook a fancy roast,
or simply a hot cross bun.

Poncho has his own built in office
which will be a delight,
as long as he doesn't work both day and night.

Ann's apartment is something else. There's
a view of the lake, a kitchen, dining room,
washer, dryer and bedroom to "boot".
If she wants solitude,
all she has to do is say, "Scoot".

May good health, happiness and
love abide with you,
in your new home with the beautiful view.

CHAPTER III
MY PHILOSOPHY ON LIFE

My Philosophy
A World In Crisis
A Love Song
Advice On Marriage
Boys and Girls
For The Love of A Dog
Friends
The Wonders Of A Dog
Global Warming
Getting to Know You – Getting to Know All About You
It's a Wonderful Life
Love
Made In America.......Oh Really?
Nature
Ode To a Spoiled Marriage
Our Nation, Then and Now
Parenthood
Perplexed

MY PHILOSOPHY

Since Emily died, I do not jog, I do not run.

What's left of my life I'm gonna have fun.

I eat what I like and drink as well.

If it cuts my life short, so what the hell!

Note: This poem is not recommended by your doctor!

A World In Crisis

I have heard, "All the world is a stage".
If so, then they should turn the page.

Iraq is a mess with Iran soon to follow,
really I find this too hard to swallow.

Global warming is even worse,
for it involves the whole Universe.

Can't be stopped? Please…just be lucid,
it's the emissions stupid.

Tons of pollutants are released every day.
If it continues there'll be hell to pay.

Whole categories of trees, plants and animals
are becoming extinct,
because man steadfastly refuses to think.

It's guess who comes next on nature's food chain,
if nothing is done about acid rain.

A Love Song

"Time after time, I tell myself that I'm
so lucky to be loving you.
So lucky to be the one you run to see,
in the evening when the day is through.
I only know what I know, the passing
years will show, we kept our love
so young, so new.
And time after time, I tell myself that I'm
so lucky to be loving you."

When Emily and I were dating,
"Time After Time"* became our theme song.

With a girl in your arms,
exuding all her charms....
and your out on the dance floor
with the one you adore...
who could ask for anything more?

With a soft musical score,
hey, what's a shoulder for?
And while you dance,
you can whisper romance,
that's not drowned out by
amplifiers you could hear in France.

Lyrics abound with tales of true love,
and marriages that are blessed from heaven above.
From, "You Are My Sunshine" to "Time After Time",
there is a real message, line after line.

Romance and love are really not the same,
and should be thought of apart.
Romance is physical but love also includes the heart.

If the words of this song reflect the relationship
between you and your wife,
you can both look forward to joy
throughout your entire married life.

*Song Title: Time After Time
Performed By: Johnny Mathis

ADVICE ON MARRIAGE

If you desire a happy marriage to
last from beginning to end—
my best advice is to "marry a friend"!
Sounds crazy? Not on your life.
It's basic to choosing a husband or a wife.

To start, you must first try to understand
what constitutes a friend.*
Once you have done this, the reason will be clear,
as to what will make your marriage last year after
year.

*A friend is............
-A person you admire and who's company you enjoy.
-A person who has many hobbies, interests and
viewpoints similar to your own.
-A friend to the very end.

BOYS AND GIRLS

Compared to a girl, a boy is easy to explain,
his interests begin with G.I. Joe and an electric train.
He likes things he can put together and take apart,
seldom things that are just plain art.
As he progresses, you can have three guesses..
football, basketball, NASCAR or pretty girls in low cut dresses.

When it comes to girls, they are more complex,
and of course, are the opposite sex.
Her interests begin with Barbie and Ken,
and shortly thereafter, think of marriage and wonder when.
They are physiologically more advanced than a boy,
and, in too many cases, will play him like a toy!

Fortunately, this scenario is rather rare,
and beautiful couples emerge with a happy life to share.
Boys will be boys and girls will be girls,
and without that-------
where would the rest of us be?

FOR THE LOVE OF A DOG

A puppy is a warm and cuddly thing,
who'll chew your slippers and everything.
He depends on you for love and affection,
and on occasion, a little confection.
Because of this, he's so easy to spoil,
whether he's a he or he's a "goil".

Disaster survivors will tell you this,
"I would not be alive, this story to tell,
if that marvelous dog hadn't picked up my smell."

Stories abound about "seeing eye" hounds,
who lead their masters to safer grounds.
Dogs, God love 'em, are loyal and smart,
and, in no time, will steal your heart.
You'll never find a truer friend,
who, no matter what, will love you to the end!

A girl once asked, "Who's smarter, a man or a woman?"
Diamonds are a girl's best friend and a dog is
man's best friend, you do the math."
A classic case of "Apples to Oranges" is what we have here,
and I contest the inference without fear.
Now girls, please don't frown...........
I've done the math and man is the smartest, "Paws Down"!

FRIENDS

As you go through life, you meet many
people along the way.
In this day and age,
some will be straight and some will be gay.
Some you're thankful for, some you're not,
but in the big picture, they're all you got!

Out of this group of people,
it's not easy to find true friends.
Some individuals go through life without any,
and it's sad because friends are jewels
and they're worth every penny!

My very dear friends are Beth and Ted.
I had a few more but now they're all dead.
This is what happens when you live too long.
Your friends start singing their final "swan song".

Nothing to do but carry on,
with precious memories of the past.
It's in this way,
old friendships are sure to last and last!

THE WONDERS OF A DOG

Dogs are totally wonderful animals who protect
and enrich our lives on a daily basis.
They come in many colors, shapes and sizes,
they are smart, talented and loyal to the end...
they are as refreshing as an oasis.

They perform many a task.
There are hunting, guide, search and rescue,
police, tracking, bomb sniffing, drug sniffing
and Eskimo sled dogs.....
properly trained, they'll do anything you ask.

Dogs are company, family and sometimes
even our children, they can also be a lot of fun.
Throw a stick and they'll retrieve it,
throw a Frisbee and they will catch it on the run.

When taken to nursing homes for periodic visits,
dogs spread joy,
it's as if someone just gave the occupants a new toy.
People who have dogs actually live longer,
their company reduces stress and makes their hearts
stronger.

Some dogs have even become movie stars,
like "Toto" and "Lassie" too,
they will play dead, roll over or "speak" right on cue.
This whole world would be an empty place,
if it were not for dogs to love and embrace!

GLOBAL WARMING

First--- a few random thoughts regarding the title of this poem:

If you think global warming is not a scare,
just go ask the nearest Polar Bear!

Be indifferent to global warming and don't lend a hand,
just stick your head in the proverbial sand!

Global warming go away,
come back again when I'm old and grey!

These thoughts would truly be funny,
if they didn't reflect the "mind set"
of so many people --- betcha-money.

We, the human race, are running out of time,
because global warming cannot be simply stopped on a dime.
To get accomplished what has to be done,
will take perseverance and dedicated scientists waiting in line.

Weather is complex and is universal.
It is germane to the existence of every living
thing on earth, in the ocean and in the sky.
If we continue to pollute our world at the current rate,
life, as we know it, will surely die.

Simply put, "If we don't get our act in "gear",
all life will totally disappear.......
how sad!

GETTING TO KNOW YOU - -
Getting To Know All About You

The title of this poem is very germane to life,
and is essential to finding a husband or a wife.

Today we have a pandemic of divorces,
brought about from different sources.
The main culprit here, I fear........
is a lack of understanding and "crying in your beer."

In my day, live-ins were not accepted too well.
They're not married so therefore will go to Hell.
Today, thank God, that archaic reasoning is gone,
giving our sons and daughters an opportunity
to "test the waters" before they move on.

When living together there are warning signs
that should never be dismissed,
especially the signs on this important list:

Is he (or she) respectful or neglectful?
Does she treat you like a "Greek God", bringing you
burnt offerings twice a day?
Does he expect you to take out the garbage?
Does he (or she) go to church only on Easter and
Christmas?
Does he take a shower Saturdays whether he needs
one or not?
Does she do all the talking?
Is he (or she) comfortable with your family and friends?
Does he change his socks everyday?

There are, of course, many more "warning flags",
too numerous to mention....
miss too many and you'll end up in detention.
I pray this little poem will enable you to have a lifetime
of good health and many a happy day.
What more could one ask for in life,
than a compatible husband or a compatible wife?

It's A Wonderful Life

As the title of this poem proclaims,
it best describes my very own.
We must not forget, however, that our lives
are really nothing but a short term loan.

The time we have on earth is very precious,
and should never be squandered.
Make the most of every day,
so your life will be fruitful in every way.
Make your life meaningful by putting
more into it than you take out.
Life, then, will be more wonderful
instead of a "testy" bout.

"Do unto others before they do unto you",
is not a healthy way to go.
A wonderful life evolves out of caring, loving,
compassion and a smile to beguile,
so if these elements are part of your life,
your spirits will soar higher than a mile!

Every now and then, give someone a hug.
I guarantee, it'll make your life feel more
wonderful than a "Bug in a rug"!

LOVE

Those who have love, one for another,
experience a real joy like no other.

Love is warm, love is caring,
love is "cool" and love is sharing.

Love is a feeling in the human heart,
which grows deeper with time and will never part.

Those in love are richer by far,
than those with jewels or a brand new car.

Love is abstract, can't be held in your hand,
but love is real and makes you feel grand.

To end this poem, though it fails to rhyme,
is the following quote, a favorite of mine.....

"Love is never having to say I'm sorry"

Made In America.....Oh, Really?

All across America cash registers are going k-ching, k-ching, k-ching,
for toys that were made in the city of Beijing!
I fully understand the rational involved here...they're cheaper,
but the effect on American manufacturers and labor,
they're the "Grim Reaper".
If you're skeptical and don't believe me,
just check out the label on the back of your DVD or TV.

The bulk of American flags are made in China, and that's sad.
They were not made in China when Granddad was a lad!

How can we in the U.S. compete? Let's face it, we can't!
Basically, their products sell,
because they're priced as cheap as hell.
We have labor laws and they do not,
a large percentage of imports are made using child labor in "sweat shops".
Toys for girls and boys, manufactured by girls and boys...how cruel,
they ought to be in school.

The latest wrinkle in this "saga" has to do with traces of lead
in toys made in China.
For this reason, there have already been two or three "recalls",
to avoid disaster before the "axe falls".

Legislation should be passed expeditiously,
requiring safety inspections prior to entry,
but this involves action by politicians and lawmakers.
Problem....some politicians, without a doubt,
are like the toys made in China,
they both need to "get the lead out!".
Until then............
you should not buy a toy that was made in Hanoi!

NATURE
**(Who'll be next in this great array?
Who will go and who will stay.)**

My family built a wonderful camp
at the north end of Brant Lake in 1939,
and have owned it ever since.
The point right on the lake is so beautiful,
that being there makes me feel like a prince.

We fought WWII hoping a better life for all,
a life of peace and prosperity and a continuance
of nature's boundless gifts to enthrall.

In the early forties, there were lots of noisy bullfrogs
and painted turtles with yellow and orange bottom shells.
Today there's not a one and other beautiful
creatures of nature are disappearing as well.

Acid rain has already taken a heavy toll
on the Adirondack trees, lakes and streams,
while, I'm afraid, some people must think
it's only happening in their dreams.

Nature itself is a food supply arranged just like a chain.
All it takes to break it is persistent "acid rain".

We've accused Iraq of having "Weapons of Mass Destruction".
In the Adirondack's, that's nothing new....
we've suffered the results of these for so many years,
we're baffled as to what to do.

In Iraq they're known as "scud" missiles...
in the Adirondacks they're power plants.
Carry this to the extreme, there'll be nothing left but ants.

ODE TO A SPOILED MARRIAGE

Don't let the title throw you,
it's not what you might think.
It's profound....partners who spoil each other,
have a union in the pink.

They never look to get their share,
their happiness is based on pleasing and care.

"What goes around, comes around", which in this case
is so true....
You spoil me and I'll spoil you.

The result is a marriage with a beautiful view!

Our Nation, Then and Now
My Thoughts

Our fore-fathers wrote "One Nation Under God!"
and with that belief, developed the greatest nation on
Earth.

Today we no longer tolerate: prayer in our schools, the
Pledge of
Allegiance with a mention of God, graduation
ceremonies which
include any reference to God, and in the near future,
"In God We Trust" will disappear from U.S. coinage.

While we true patriots were "asleep at the switch", it is
now permissible to burn the flag we formally pledged
our allegiance to and sang songs about.
One of these, in fact, is our National Anthem......

"Gave proof through the night that our flag was still
there"
"It's a grand old flag, it's a high flying flag"
"Hooray for the red, white and blue"

The words to these great songs were inspirational.
They spoke of respect and loyalty for our laws as
originally written.

Our heritage and original values are steadily eroding
away and we seem powerless to stop it.
No wonder our nation and indeed, the entire world,
is "going to hell in a hand basket!"

I've hoped, throughout my entire life, that I would see a
world better off than when I came into it......guess it
was
only a dream turned into a veritable nightmare!

PARENTHOOD

Having children is a planned affair,
sometimes true...sometimes not.
In either case, you're on the spot,
and must give it all you've got.

Unfortunately there are no books
or owners manual,
that advises you on how to raise a Diane or Daniel.

In the animal species, when babies are due,
the male instinctively knows what to do.
In the human species, he hasn't a clue,
so birthing classes are designed for you.

Newborns are a sight to behold,
and totally cuddly so I'm told.
When the chores begin to kick in,
your patience becomes, at best, very thin.

Before the arrival there are baby showers,
which sometimes go on for many hours.
Face the facts, babies are expensive to have and to hold,
and usually this continues until they become quite old.

All of this pales in the light of the love and joys,
we parents receive from our little girls and boys.

The next phase is grandchildren with
charm and grace.
As someone once said,
"If I'd known how much fun they are,
we would have had them in the first place!"

PERPLEXED

"Peace on earth good will to men"
The whole world seems to go from bad to worse
so I'm wondering when.

I have prayed for, at least a semblance of peace
in the Middle East for years,
but, in reality, there has only been escalating
hatred, death and tears.

I thank you, God, for beautiful springtime
and sunshiny days,
but when it comes to natural disasters,
I'm totally left in a daze.

When newspapers and television report crime is down,
they must mean it's down the street or down the alley.
In either case it's too high a tally.

Global warming is being caused by air pollution,
emitted from factories, power plants, cars or a bus,
I guess the ultimate culprit in the end, has got to be us.

Dear Lord God, our planet has become a scary place,
too much to handle by the human race.
One must seek solace through their faith in you,
otherwise, Lord, there's really nothing left for us to do.

CHAPTER IV
SEASONS AND HOLIDAYS

Happy New Year
Winter
Valentines Day
Set Your Clocks Ahead
Spring The Awakening – The New Birth
Easter is Really Not About Bunnies
Summer
The Fourth of July
Fall
Thanksgiving
The Wonder of Christmas
Home for The Holidays
A New Slant on Christmas!
The Greatest Story Ever Told
Christmas, A Heavenly Time

HAPPY NEW YEAR

It's out with the old and in with the new,
which is just fine unless you're ninety two!

December 31st is New Year's Eve, where there's
lots of parties, wild hats, noise makers and glitter in the hair.
If the truth be known, you appreciate the
invitation and you're glad to be there.

The main event, of course, is in Times Square,
where thousands of revelers have come from everywhere.
The anticipation of a brand new year is
manifested by the noise that's in the air.

As midnight approaches, all eyes are on the ball,
and excitement increases as it begins to fall,
5 – 4 – 3 – 2 – 1   Happy New Year!

Good wishes abound,
with plenty of hugs and kisses to go around.
So as a nation, old troubles are, at least for the
moment, set aside.
It is a chance at a new beginning,
and, as well, a renewed pride.

If mankind would only work for good, not bad,
this cockeyed world could be better by far.
It's worth a try....I'm "game" if you are!

Winter
A Cold Reception

I can understand the attraction to ski,
but quite frankly, it's too damn cold for me!
Downhill slalom looks to be swell,
until you realize they're going down the
mountainside like a bat out-a-hell.

Winter is fabulous if you like "long johns", cold hands
and feet
and unbelievably high cost of fuel oil heat.
Winter is also nice,
if you don't mind a lot of snow, hail and damnable ice.

When listening to the "Weather Channel" and they tell you
there's a mass of Arctic air moving down from
Canada—it's not good news.
Temperatures of 15 degrees with a chill factor of 8,
is enough to give anyone a case of the blues.

I hate being negative, but when it comes to
Winter I honestly must say,
I look forward to seeing the first red robin
and getting rid of that damn old sleigh!

VALENTINE'S DAY

Of all the special days in the year, Valentine's Day is
the only one that celebrates love between two human
beings, one for another.
It's not the love of a dress, a suit or a porch with a swing.
Love is from your heart and soul – it's the dozen red roses,
a box of chocolates or a "mushy" card type of thing.

Like the Alamo, Valentine's Day should never be forgotten.
It speaks of love and all things good, not all things rotten.
The expression "It's better to give than it is to receive"
is never more true,
than on Valentine's Day when you say, "I love you".

Valentine's Day is a chance to "step up to the plate",
and express your love to your girlfriend, boyfriend or mate.
In these busy, stressful days, when was the last time
you told
your wife how much she means to you and how much
you really care?
Life is surprisingly short so let her know how you feel.
I'll bet dollars to donuts, you'll come out ahead on the deal!

SET YOUR CLOCKS AHEAD

Daylight saving time is a very good friend of mine.
The days get longer, the sun gets stronger and the robins arrive,
to make us glad to be alive.
Days and nights become warmer, shrubs and trees begin to bud and suddenly, "puff",
as if by magic -----no more of that white stuff.

It's such a treat, to wake up in the morning with the sun's rays in your eyes,
as you contemplate having coffee, scrambled eggs and good old "home fries".
Your evenings too, are such a delight,
you don't come home in the dark,
as if it were the middle of the night.

I believe God made winter with all its snow and ice,
so we can look forward to spring and everything nice!

SPRING, THE AWAKENING – THE NEW BIRTH

Spring is a most beautiful time of the year,
when "Old Man Winter" is gone and daffodils appear.
Trees and bushes start to explode their buds,
and red robins begin feeding on worms and grubs.

Spring is a harbinger of nature's re-birth,
and another chance for mankind to start anew-
just like the trees and flowers do.
"Mother Nature" gives us a lesson each year—
to let bygones be bygones and emerge free and clear.

Spring is a time when farmers seed,
so they can raise crops that people need.
Our food chain is vital to continuing re-birth,
and the means to that end is found in the earth.

Spring is fresh and clean,
like taking a shower, if you know what I mean.
Shortly thereafter you'll be smelling the roses,
with all of the beauty that composes.

Whenever you feel "blue" and this crazy world is
getting to you—think about Springtime with all
it's newness and grace.
It just might remove the frown from your face
and bring forth a smile to take it's place!

Easter Is Really Not About Bunnies

The crucified Christ was placed in a tomb
with a huge stone for a seal.
Three days later the stone had been moved,
Christ was gone, and that's unreal.

The miracle herein is that Christ had risen,
and could not be held in any form of prison.
He died for our sins and took them away,
that's why Easter is such a glorious day.

Christ appeared before his twelve disciples
for the last supper in the upper room.
It was there he asked them to both eat the bread
and drink the wine as a remembrance of him.
The name of this celebration is "Communion",
which Christians 'round the world partake in unison.

And Easter, like Christmas, should be celebrated
with the true meaning in mind,
not just fancy bonnets, Easter baskets
and things of that kind.

We love you Lord for all you have done,
and as our Savior, you're the only one!

SUMMER
(The Lazy, Hazy Days!)

Summer is a happy, carefree time of the year.
It's the season of vacations, walks in the park,
beach parties and beer.
On the 4th of July the parades abound,
and if it doesn't rain you can take out your hound.

Farmer's fields are loaded with corn stalks and such,
that at harvest time, is never too much.
We are blessed in the U.S.A. with food for our people,
and for our horses, an abundance of hay.
As it was true in the past, it's true today,
"Make hay while the sun shines" is what they say!

Summer is the "outdoor" season,
that invites you there for any reason.
There are many for both woman and man,
and heading the list would be getting a tan.
Swimming, tennis and golf are close seconds to be enjoyed,
when warm Summer weather is generously deployed.

Summer traffic you could do without.
It fosters "road rage", "aggressive driving"
and an occasional bout.
It's important to be careful when you drive,
just to be sure you stay alive.
And make certain you "buckle-up",
or you might be "pushing" the buttercups up.

I, for one, also enjoy Summer a lot.
My only complaint that I don't hesitate to tell,
Is when the temperature rises
and gets hotter than the "Hinges of Hell"!

THE FOURTH OF JULY

The Colonists felt oppressed,
by taxes that could not be addressed.
The "Boston Tea Party" was an effective demonstration,
against these taxes without representation.

The War of Independence began on July 4, 1776,
while the British had a professional army,
the Colonists had a "rag-tag" mix.

To track the British, a signal light atop Old North Church,
was positioned so all could see....
one if by land and two if by sea.

When the war began, it was a scary time,
and no news came via "America On Line".
It's hard to imagine, of course,
that in those days it came from a man on a horse.

To be more specific, it was Paul Revere who alerted
them all from town to town..
He shouted out loud for all to hear,
including those who were deaf or had a "tin ear".

The British were seasoned troops,
led by a boy drummer in front of men
in red coats and wearing black boots.

The Colonists fought from behind the trees,
while the colorful British were out in the open,
the front row down on their knees.
In the War of Independence, George Washington
got much of the glory,
but other great leaders as well,
played a part in this magnificent story.

Betsy Ross, who wanted nothing to lag,
sat right down and created a flag.
Thirteen stars and stripes too,
told the story in red, white and blue.

This flag is yours and mine,
and has withstood the test of time.
It represents the land of the free,
and there again, that's you and me.

On October 19, 1781, General Cornwallis surrendered
at Yorktown, Virginia in the last major
battle of the Revolutionary War.

The 4th of July is near at hand,
with fireworks, majorettes and a host of great bands.
And so, the 4th of July is a joyous occasion,
that is celebrated by a most grateful nation.

Fall
(A Breath of Fresh Air)

Tulips, roses and a myriad of other pretty
flowers abound in Spring.
In Summer we enjoy days at the beach,
ice cream, sodas and lazy days on the swing.
Summers are really wonderful, except during
prolonged "heat waves", they turn into "bummers".
And the "dog days" of August are very hard to take,
unless you have access to a delightfully
cool fresh water lake.
Central air is terrific if you have it, providing,
of course, you can see your way clear to afford it.

Mother Nature must sense our plight and hears our
call,
for before we know it, she's turned it into Fall---
all dressed up in magnificent colors of foliage
that's enjoyed by us all.

Fall is literally a breath of fresh air,
with it's balmy days and cool nights for everyone to
share.

Fall is also a busy time for wildlife.
Squirrels begin burying nuts and other foods around,
to be retrieved later on when snow covers the ground.
Clouds of blackbirds darken the skies,
swooping from field to field.
Huge flocks of geese heading south in "V" formations,
tell us all it's time to plan our Winter vacations.

When it comes to Seasons, I think out of all---
September, October and November, are probably
the most interesting, most comfortable and
most exciting months that, when grouped together,
we recognize as Fall!

THANKSGIVING
(Amen)

When the Pilgrims landed, they needed a dock,
for lack of another name they called it Plymouth Rock.

Before they could settle there was work to begin.
Trees to fell and cabins to build
with walls that were thick, not too thin.

The Pilgrims were so very right
when they said, "Come sit down and we'll have a bite".

The whole colony came to feast on turkey, corn and stew,
the Indians were invited too.
The men hunted and provided the meat,
the women cooked, I think that's neat.

The Indians brought a lot of corn,
which the Pilgrims hadn't seen since the day they were born.

This celebration was a show of Thanksgiving,
to thank God for a new beginning.
One thing though, seems a little bit quirky,
everyone was thankful except the poor turkey!

THE WONDER OF CHRISTMAS
(Wonder what it is – Wonder what it means)

At Christmas time we celebrate Christ's birth,
the most important event ever on earth.

God's son came down for you and me
so we might have life eternally.

Never has there been so great a love,
which can only come from God above.

Believe the Christmas story, believe it in your heart.
Without any question, God will do his part.

Christmas is a time of joy,
when we gather to honor the heavenly boy.

Too bad more people don't see the light
from the star that twinkled that special night.

HOME FOR THE HOLIDAYS

The holiday season for those alone is, for many,
a psychological nightmare.
We know full well what we've been told,
"Pick up your life and move on!"
Seems simple enough but not if it's your
life long love whose gone.

Speaking for myself, I really don't know what I'd do,
if I had no family, friends and neighbors such as I do.
Along these lines, you don't have to search too far,
to find souls who are much worse off than you are.

Depression is a rotten thing,
your feelings go numb and everything.
Only you, with a proper mind-set, can ultimately
make it go away,
allowing you to return to a more normal life of
love and joy and a happy holiday!

A New Slant On Christmas!

Christmas is a joyous time of the year,
when we celebrate with families and sing songs of good cheer.
The Christmas story offers a promise of salvation,
which is available to all regardless of their station.

The power of Christmas transcends logic when we hear,
Frosty The Snowman, Charlie Brown and the Three
Chipmunks sing praises each year.
The melodies themselves are so pleasing to the ear,
until Alvin sings, of course, he's the sour one, I fear.

Question: If the afore mentioned singers,
who supposedly are not real,
make Christmas, which is real,
have so much appeal,
then how can so many resist accepting what the
Lord has promised in his "Heavenly deal"?

THE GREATEST STORY EVER TOLD

It was a virgin birth
that brought God's only son here to earth.
Born in a stable with cows and sheep
and rocked in a cradle to put him to sleep.

No one knew exactly who he was,
except three wise men traveling far,
being guided along by a twinkling star.
They brought gifts of myrrh, frankincense and gold,
to honor the Savior who was there as they were told.
Shepherds, too, followed the same light,
that shone so bright on that heavenly night.

Christ's time on earth was like no other,
he was a preacher, teacher and performed
miracles too many to cover.
He came to forgive our iniquities and to save
all souls who believed in him.
Christ promised us a place in Heaven,
where all believers enter devoid of sin.
There's never been a promise so profound, so unique,
that includes the opportunity for us all
to reach the heavenly peak.

He was born in a stable and died on a cross.
Alpha to Omega is what the Greeks would say,
yet the time between is the real story,
of Christ in all his glory.
As one reads the bible and things unfold,
you come to the realization that it is....
THE GREATEST STORY EVER TOLD.

*I dedicate this poem to God who helped me write it.

CHRISTMAS, A HEAVENLY TIME

Christmas is for celebrating the birth of our
savior Jesus Christ and a spirit of giving as well.
God sent his only son as a gift for all and maybe, just maybe,
the tradition of gift giving began.....hard to tell.

Because of what God has done,
makes it more blessed to give than receive.
It also generates wild anticipation on Christmas Eve.

Christmas morning is excitement time.
We gather as a family and wonder which
beautifully wrapped package is really mine.

After the "cats are out of the bag",
we sit 'round the table eating good food
that's certain to make your middle sag.

Christmas day is many things to many people,
but to our family, it's a celebration of Christ's birth,
with unending prayers for peace on earth.

Amen

CHAPTER V
A SMATTERING OF HUMOR

A Labor Of Love
Buy, Sell or What?
Cell Phones
Christmas 2006
Cooking Is Not A "Piece of Cake"
Death
Diets
Headstone
In The Red
My Plumber, Ray
My "Take" on Rock
Ode to Confidence?
Old Age----Who Me?
Sex
Snippets of Old Age
Taxed To The Max
The "Tin Lizzy" and Me
My Happy Poem

A Labor Of Love

Taxes on our camp at Brant Lake have risen so high,
we either had to rent or sell.
And sell was really not an option,
for that would have been hell!

Over a period of sixty plus years,
At-Last-A-Camp has become a family "keepsake"
that holds happy memories for us all.
It's for that reason we rent it the entire Summer
season up until the Fall.

When you become a landlord you inherit
responsibilities that require a lot of work.
Given our purpose, we all lovingly
toil without even a single shirk.

We go up a week in the Spring and again in the Fall,
camp to clean and a dock to install.
It's a family thing that combines quality
time with having lots of fun.
And all things we accomplish are truly worth a ton!

Buy, Sell or What?

If your concern is about investments,
and you don't know whether to buy or sell,
these hard decisions can be a real living hell.

Wilmington Brokerage gives you all the facts,
which will produce profits for you...
not just marginally but to the max.

Their brokers are of professional grade,
and at times of stress will come to your aid.
They are patient and kind....
ask a dumb question, they don't mind!

High rollers and guys like me,
get treated with the utmost of dignity.
My personal advisor is Ms. Mereider,
whose grasp on the market,
you'd swear she was an insider.

She's smart, she's wise, she's cute,
and a super human being to boot!

CELL PHONES

The cell phone is a marvelous thing,
some take pictures and everything.
To let you know there's a call coming in,
it plays tunes from rock to opera---
what happened to the "ring"?

Unfortunately, the cell phone has a drawback or two.
In a public place, with people close by,
there are no secrets, personal or business,
no matter how you try.

Using the cell phone while you drive a car
should be strictly taboo,
the next fatality might be you!
Here's good advice------
If you must use the phone while you drive,
just take a moment and pull to the side.

These days, paying close attention to the road
while you're behind the wheel,
is made more difficult by far,
by the many "extras" that are in the car.
Besides cell phones, there are stereos, radios,
satellite positioning and DVD TV.
That's a bit too much if you're asking me!

To enjoy a safe ride from beginning to end,
attention and patience is a winning blend.

CHRISTMAS 2006

I went to Walmart a while ago......
I hate that damn store but the prices are low.

First off, shopping itself is no lark----
it's a pain in the ass just trying to park.

After shopping and checking out,
I left through the exit door,
only to find myself face to face
with cars galore.

Damn! --- did I park down isle six, five or two?
I should always remember but for me that's hard to do.

There must be an answer to this re-occurring
parking dilemma, but what?
After much searching, I came across the perfect solution.

Seeing as how Diane, Barbara and Christine
do most of the buying,
I'm giving each a gift which, to me,
is on the leading edge of electronics, no lying!

COOKING IS NOT A "PIECE OF CAKE"

At the dinner table I can carve,
but if I had to do the cooking, I would surely starve.
I'm in awe of people like Julia Childs,
James Beard and Emeril Lagasse,
but frozen dinner by Stouffers is,
"kicking it up a notch" for me!

Most of my recipes I get from a can
and most of these are cooked in a pan.
If I happen to see a recipe with no more than
three ingredients, I might try it,
but if it's anything I can get at the store,
like" Hamburger Helper", I'll buy it.
I can boil water and toast marshmallows,
after that not much else follows.

Given my penchant for the culinary arts,
there is one appliance that my very life does save...
and that's the incredible microwave.
It heats my coffee and among other things,
it cooks my dinner.
In my kitchen that makes it a genuine winner!

DEATH

It's not the cough that carries you off...
it's the coffin they carry you off in!
Death is definitely a finite condition,
I don't even like the prone position.
In life, prone is synonymous with rest,
but in death it's a convenience at the very best.

The signs of death are easy to spot,
whether you are a doctor or not.
In death there is no movement or pain,
as to weight, there is no loss or gain.
This fact is a dieter's dream,
it allows them to eat to the ultimate extreme.

Pall bearers should all be your debtors*--money due.
All your life you carried them, now they can carry you!

*Debtors, themselves, do not have to be buried—
they're already in the "hole"

DIETS

There are more diets than you can shake a stick at.
They all say you can lose weight and still eat
three prescribed meals a day.
So can a horse if he only eats hay.
Listen to the ads ---many are hard to believe.
"Don't eat meat, don't eat starches,
get too heavy and you'll develop fallen arches".

Keep track of your weight when losing pounds,
but at the same time, remain strong.
Don't forget the Holocaust diet was one that went
horribly wrong.

There are people who appear to have an inner-tube
around their waist and a table above their rump,
that should go on a diet or use a fat pump.
More to be pitied than censored I guess,
just going to the bathroom must be a challenge to
success.

At the food store these same people will use an
electric cart, which is kinda neat,
but when they get on it, you can't even find the seat.

I've always been suspicious of going on a diet ---
just the first syllable prevents me from trying it!

HEADSTONE

A headstone is a marker at best.
It indicates where a body's at rest.

At least I know a body is there,
instead of ashes thrown in the air.

Other than that it serves no purpose,
I took my love home right after the service!

In The Red

There is a very special group of people,
who in fact are in the red,
we're not talking money,
we're talking about their head!

Their numbers are dwindling year after year,
and in time will be extinct, I truly do fear.

Just 4% of the world's population carries the red hair gene,
a sad fact for sure,
'Cause red heads to me have so much allure.

My great granddaughter, Madison, is a red head,
and smart as a whip,
conversing with her is really a trip.

To all red heads I want to say,
Whenever we meet, you make my day!

My Plumber, Ray

Plumbing problems? Don't pull your hair,
just call Ray and he'll be there.

He's prompt, efficient and neat,
and can fix anything from a kitchen sink
to a wobbly toilet seat.

Ray is honest and fair and when the job is done,
whether he replaced or installed,
you'll certainly be glad it was him you called!

My Take On Rock

Music of the current generation,
sounds more to me like degeneration.

Now, right up front, I'll have to admit,
if I can't hum it, whistle it or dance to it...
I don't like it!

Every Rock concert I see on "TV" has a male lead singer
with long shaggy hair and "way out" pants.
He seems oblivious to who else is on stage,
as he gyrates and plays his guitar while doing a dance.

Each group has it's own style, which involves
screeching into a half swallowed microphone.
The girl leads are not much better,
sexy I'll admit and they know how to groan.

You can hear Rock bands playing in night clubs and bars,
but the music sounds more like a hog calling
contest with waitresses from "Hooters" as stars.

When Rock fans stop beside you on the street,
you'd swear they had a bass drum in the back seat.

In the future, I fear,
they'll no longer have the ability to hear.
That will be the price they have paid,
but hey, there's still the hearing aid.

I'm sorry girls and boys,
but Rock sounds to me like illiterate lyrics set to noise!

ODE TO CONFIDENCE?

If only mankind had any class,
they'd work together and get their heads out of their a...

When will we ever face the real world's trouble,
religious jealousies, greed and the power struggle.

Millions of people die every day,
while others are out "making hay".
This creates a hot bed of trouble,
that requires very little to break the bubble.

Given what mankind has done in the past,
I believe I too will put my head up my a..!!

OLD AGE ---- WHO ME?

At 21 you think of playing games
and having some fun.
At 87 you're so damn tired,
you can hardly run.

I have found a few "perks" in being old,
but they come at a terrible price.
"Handicap" parking spaces
and "Senior Discounts" are quite nice,
but just crossing the street
can be a toss of the dice.

In old age, health problems abound,
not the least of which is hearing sound.
People will say you need a hearing aid,
but they cost a pile of chips.
In this situation, your best bet would
be learning to read other's lips.

Signs of old age are many,
you can thank your lucky stars if you haven't any...

Walk to the far end of the house and don't have a clue
as to why you're there.
Make a list of things to do, then can't find the list.
Spend 15 minutes looking for your glasses, then
suddenly realize you have them on.
Your spouse sends you to the food store and then pins
the list to the lapel of your coat.

There are many more examples of aging I could
mention,
but unfortunately I have no memory retention.

In my humble opinion, old age is just like an
Electrolux...
it just plain sucks!

SEX

People ask me if sex is an issue.
My eyes well up and I grab for a tissue!

It's sad...now if I had the chance,
I'd have to leave it in my pants!

God is good, God is great,
just too bad I can no longer mate!

SNIPPETS OF OLD AGE
(Please Don't Laugh---Your Turn's Next!)

When someone asks you, "When's your birthday?"
You say, "July 7th"
They say, "What year?"
And because you can't remember, you say,
"Every year!"

Hearing Aids

The cheapest one is a sign hung around your neck that reads:
"Speak up!"

Your wife has to remind you:
"The turn signal's still on!"

A man thought young girls were whistling at him until he realized it was only his hearing aid!

Other Tell-Tale Signs

You write notes to yourself, then forget to look at them.

You know who Guy Lombardo is.

If you know who Enrico Carruso was, you should get your important papers
together and review your Living Will.

You ogle at girls just to keep up with the latest style in skirts.

You used to chase girls but now it's only in your dreams.
Look on the bright side—in your dreams, you can still catch 'em.

Who said, "One gets better with age?"
Maybe wine, but not you!

And when it comes down to "face lifts", Viagra and "tummy tucks",
you'll realize that "old age" really "SUCKS!"

TAXED TO THE MAX?
(Dedicated to Linda)

April rain may bring May flowers,
but to taxpayers it brings nothing but pain for hours and hours.

Time gets short as we prepare for that frightening day,
when forms are due or there's hell to pay.

If at night you toss and turn,
it's probably caused by your tax return.

You may try a C.P.A., my friend,
but this'll cost you "big time" in the end.

The forms themselves are so confusing,
they make no sense and are not amusing.

We pay directly through the nose,
and are very lucky they don't take our clothes.

If you're smart and want to stay out of hock,
you had better go around to see H&R Block!

THE TIN LIZZY AND ME

When I came off the assembly line,
my lungs were strong and my heart was fine.

And now, years later-------
My starter is weak and so is my alternator!
My tires are getting bald, just look and see,
and I'm losing my grip on reality.

My seats are badly worn,
But hey, I still have a melodious horn.
Brakes are another matter---
whenever I apply them, the pedestrians scatter!

All of this nonsense is no big deal,
except when I'm behind the wheel!
I hate to admit that I look like a slob,
who is badly in need of a Macco paint job!

MY HAPPY POEM

Many poems are stiff and serious.
I find many are also mysterious.

Some speak of love and some of death,
and many sound like re-runs of Macbeth.

And who am I to criticize?
I'm sorry but I'll not apologize.

I much prefer the lighter vain,
dealing with sunshine and not with pain.

With this thought in mind,
I wrote a poem about my life,
that speaks not of sorrow, nor of strife,
I call it My Happy Poem.

Happy to be loved by loved ones,
and happy to be alive.
Happy that God , so far,
has enabled me to survive.

I'm happy about the life I've lived,
with all the perks along the way.
There are so many blessings God has given me,
that truly made my day.
And just knowing you do hear me, Lord,
makes me happy when I pray!

.... and away we go!

Printed in the United States
120846LV00003BA/63/P